Y0-BLT-649

Under a Toenail Moon

Terry M Gresham

T&T Press

Lawton, Oklahoma

2015

Special Thanks to the Cameron University Sigma Tau Delta
Poetry group for support and assistance.

Under a Toenail Moon

Copyright 2015 By Terry Gresham. All Rights Reserved.

No part of this book may be performed, recorded, or otherwise transmitted without the written consent of the author and the permission of the publisher.

Request for permission should be addressed to:

Terry M Gresham
801 NW Dearborn Ave
Lawton. Oklahoma
73507

Cover Photo Copyright 2014 by Terry Gresham

Introduction by Teri McGrath

A shiny medallion of a memory I have of the open poetry readings when they used to be held at the coffee shop/used book store, Forgotten Works, is of a time when Terry Gresham walked up to the stage and recited what he said was a Jim Morrison poem, called "THE SKY." The poem went like this: The Sky. Of course there was much more to the poem than that. There was the room and the mood of the room, which was --somber, let's say. Often poetry readings can be somber because poets are pretty deep and sometimes sad people. And then to make the poem happen, I think, the reader needed to be Terry Gresham, which involved having longish, crazyish black hair and sparkly black eyes and some cool jacket. (And maybe a hat? I don't remember. I like to think he was wearing a hat) It definitely meant standing to the side of the microphone and speaking directly to the audience. And saying, "The SKY," in a really cool way while gesturing with your arm in the direction of the sky, as if you made it. Or as if you're introducing it to a friend. The point is there is more to the poem than just saying the words. Certainly at a poetry reading this is true.

And when I met with Terry the other night to discuss how awesome I think he is, he told me that I am right about that. He said that back then, when he first started going to the poetry reading, he could see it "needed livening up a little bit." At those readings, he says, laughing, "You had to have so much meaning.
You know, your heart had to be, like — out there."

What he was trying to do with his poetry was something different from what he was hearing, something that got away from sentimentality—"or even feeling," he said, not necessarily referring to the efforts I made back then. Or, for that matter, the efforts I make now to be deep and feelingful. "Well, it's not that that's not good poetry," he says. "You know, I'm a ham, anyway. When you're out in public, it ought to be a little entertaining."

Humor is an important element to Terry's work and one of the ways he forms a connection with his audience and opens them up. For instance, in "My Dream and Me," the speaker dreams of a world from which "all / idiots had vanished." The world seems to be a better place:

> "There were celebrations. / People liked it."

But the speaker is glad it is only a dream because he cannot find himself in that world. He has vanished with the other idiots. A lot of Terry's poems work this way—they comment in some way on human nature using humor and some self-deprecation. And the poems ring true, in part, because he so easily and deliberately reveals himself behind the words but, perhaps more importantly, because he reveals the reader, too. As members of his audience at a reading we can often literally see ourselves in his work, as he lists John Morris, Rob and Weyodi Duncan, Sam McMichael and other regular attendees among his influences, along with Joy Harjo, John Lennon and Steve Allen.

Another special connection Terry has with his audience at the readings is that much of his inspiration comes from what he hears and sees here in Lawton. Sitting at Hoffman's one night, he hears the bartender say, "It's way after midnight, baby!" Or driving down 11th street, he sees a balloonless ribbon tied to a fence. And these things he makes into poetry. So some of the laughter you will hear when Terry is reading is not a response to a funny line or idea, but a plain expression of delight in shared experiences — if only in the shared experience of the poem. Terry Gresham reads his poetry as if he is discovering it for the first time. He laughs at some of his lines. He sometimes stumbles because he is unable to read the new lines or revisions 7 he's scribbled onto the page just before getting up to read. He clearly loves words and the act of composing. He loves reading, and his delight is contagious. As we talked, the other night, Terry recited some lines from a poem called "d'Ordinare" (ordinary things sound more interesting in French, he says):

> "One day, I would like to be like a song
> and I want Annie Lennox to sing me.
> I would love to be notable like that."

The lines, I think, are beautiful — sweet and surprising. And what made them even more charming was the way he laughed after every one of them. Terry Gresham's poetry is always surprising and always delightful. He works to pleasantly unsettle the audience from any expectations we might have. He says, "I try to think of the words on the page as not being the most important thing about the piece. Like a DNA or a protein molecule that has a primary structure (words) a secondary structure (words folding upon other words) and a tertiary structure (how the poem coils even further around due to its environment) I like to have the poem doing biology and somersaults. I like to have the poem doing things that it shouldn't." When Terry took the stage at the poetry reading, he wasn't necessarily the first to introduce levity to the event, but he is especially good at it. He is humorous, mischievous and engaging. Though the readings have changed venue several times, they are still going strong in large part because of the strong sense of community writers like Terry help to create.

This article first appeared in the November issue of the Okie Magazine, 2009.

Contents

- No One Steps Across this Line
- Know thyself
- Chili
- Under a Toenail Moon
- The Art of Not Caring
- Cats of Our Lives
- I Do Not Remember Dancing
- John Lennon's Carpenter
- Walk Like the Sun
- Too Much Imagination
- The Life of Me
- At is Ket. At a Sket.
- Pie
- How to Offend a Fish
- Great
- Friend
- On Sunday
- Garbage Can
- My Dream and Me
- Ignes Fatui
- Notes of October
- Saturn
- Moon and Star
- The Herman Imbroglio
- Anaconda Freak 'em Caster
- Women
- D'ordinaire
- Still Life with a Cat
- Then On That Same Night
- Fall to the Ground

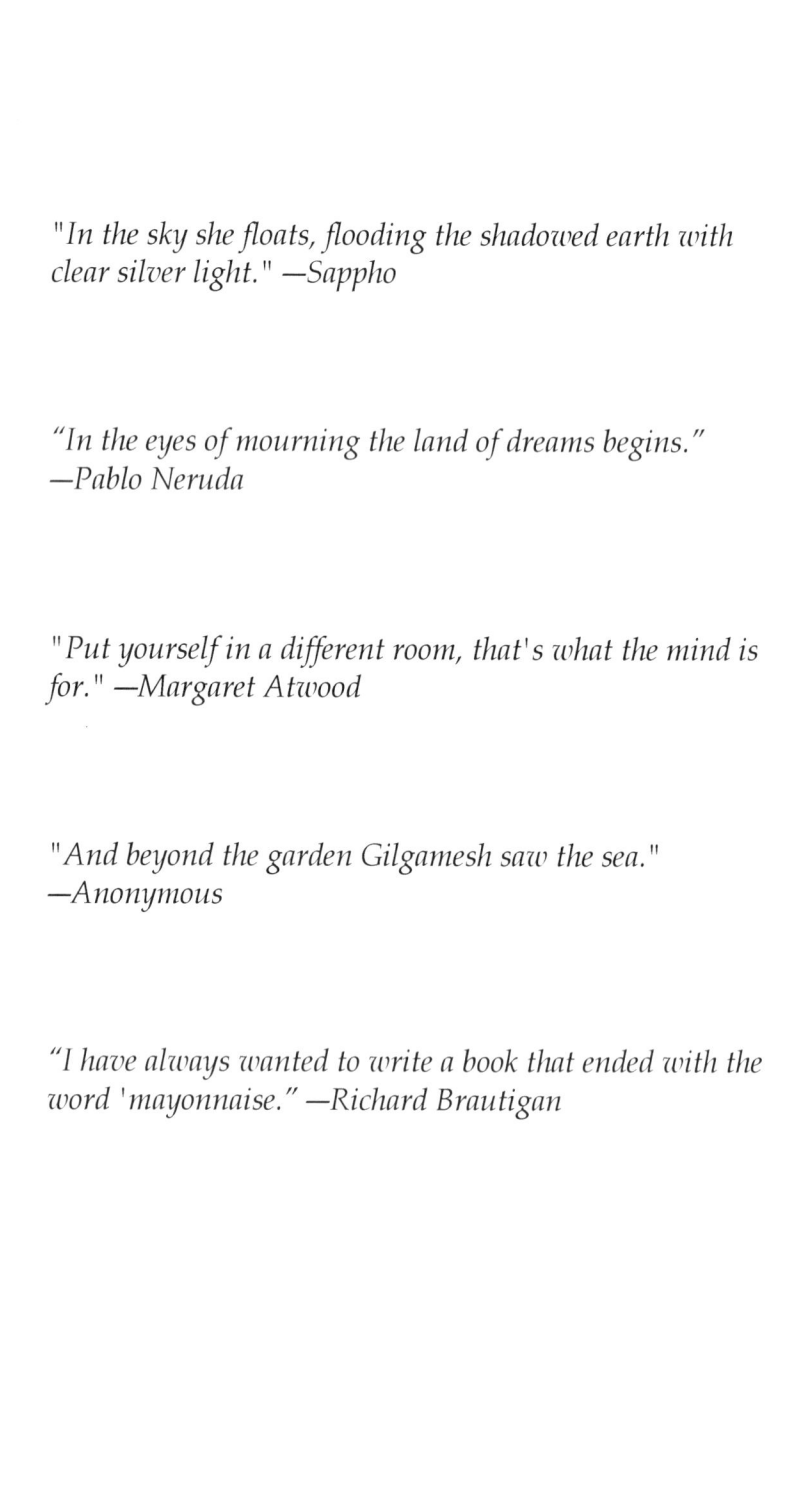

"In the sky she floats, flooding the shadowed earth with clear silver light." —Sappho

"In the eyes of mourning the land of dreams begins." —Pablo Neruda

"Put yourself in a different room, that's what the mind is for." —Margaret Atwood

"And beyond the garden Gilgamesh saw the sea." —Anonymous

"I have always wanted to write a book that ended with the word 'mayonnaise.'" —Richard Brautigan

No One Steps Across this Line

No One Steps Across this Line.
Well, okay, you may, reader,
but you might have to eat some of the pizza
I'm working on.

I can write in a slice or two for you
— if you will let me.

I once studied the chair and desk of Whitman while I
stood behind a sectioning off rope.
There, I hungered to sit at that desk and write for
Walt a pepperoni —
thick dough crust poem with extra cheese extra olives.

But I could not. Even in his house, I could not cross
that line. That's fine since I did not know what Walt
would drink: Coke or Pepsi.

Still, don't it go that existence seems spent
on either this side or that side of a line.

We are line junkies — or linemen riding fences
in wide sectioned off counties.

No one steps across this line and
no one better step across that line.
I'm so glad my mind's on the inside my head
or I would lose it. Then where would I be?

So what, pray tell, shall we say about the soul
who steps outside station, looses restraint,
then chases a great hunger? And who
crosses over the great sea?

Later tonight I'm gonna sit right down any ol' place
and write myself a pizza with everything I want on it.
And you, dear reader, are welcome to join me.

Cross that line. Feel free.

Or
have I gone too far, crossed some sort of line
suggesting that
you, Whitman, and I share snacks?

I don't need to have olives. I'll write them out

—if you will let me.

What's that you say?

Doesn't Walt want olives?

Am I the only one?

Know Thyself

Be a first rate version of yourself, not a second rate version of someone else. — Judy Garland

Nothing
but gray skies today after so many cold blue.

Spring
has been waiting to start doing her
stuff around here — tapping her foot —
for several weeks now.

I told her I would do
what I could do.

So, I yelled at winter
for I don't know how long using
language
not fit for any church.

But now all
I got to take and show to spring
are these gray skies
winter handed to me
as he threw me out
his door.

I'm thinking that in the future
I will let spring wait.

I am just a mere man —
I am not too good at negotiating
with seasons.

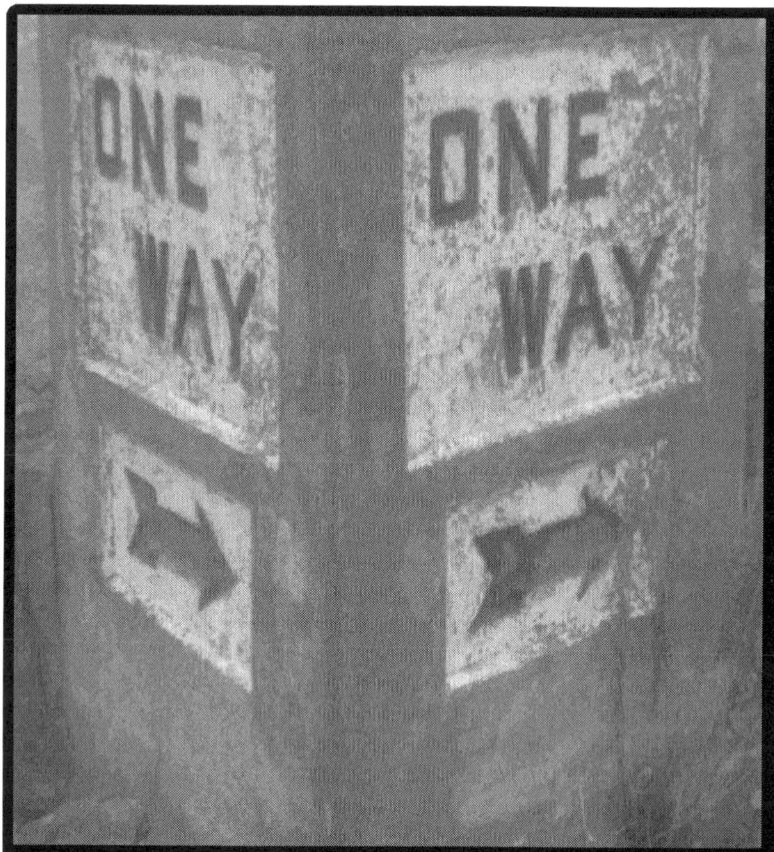
ONE
WAY
ONE
WAY

Chili

I
handed
the
world
to
her

like a hot bowl of chili.

She
handed
it
back
to
me

like a hot bowl of chili con carne.

I said, "Chili is chili."

"No, it's not," she said,

as if I was supposed to add
meat to the metaphor
I had given her concerning
the world.

I went on to ask her
if she was thinking
of the country

Chile —

a country of southwest
South America with a long
coastline.

Or

was she thinking
about chili —

a highly spiced dish made
from red peppers,
meat, and often beans.

She said, "Yes."

From that moment on
I decided it was best
to always

hand
her the world
as if it were
the world like a plate.

This way she can add anything she wants.

Under a Toenail Moon

Way high above
and way high down below
inside every stone
and flapping bird wing
in every beginning step in deep fog
atop some soggy cracker in a tin
leaps your alligator skin and teeth
beneath Venus
under a sea of time

               —a sea of time.

It is the pine cone scent and broken sun
the smiles of children unwashed in spring
about spinning dancers inside music
in Brahmsian tunes and shuffling cards
much like lovers hands touching nose and toes
beneath clover
under piles of chocolate

               —piles of chocolate.

Our fate is like plaster as it pours.
It's sealed and cured by waiting
same as your sour throat.
Strength is only not going it alone.

Wish we could wish upon a wish, but no,
hope is our tormentor and we are molded
beneath old stars
under wires of grass

               —wires of grass.

Now a camera flash and a gush of steam
a dreamer's dream, the song of the mosquito
16 miles below the Cumberland Gap.
And we are burlap. We live like turpentine.
Our pen draws a fine line — you, me and us
— beneath a pulse
under a toenail moon

                      — a toenail moon.

The Art of Not Caring

Started out only
nodding
and sticking out my tongue.

Then I began waving
both hands

now

like I just don't care.
That must have been the reason

she began
yelling the same
thing over
and over
at me,

"What the heck are you doing over there?"
she said.

I said, "And I don't care.

Jimmy crack corn and I don't care.
That's in a song,"

I contended.

At times, I think I make her go mad

just so we will
have something to talk about.

"Every little once in a while.
Oh no, that's in a song, too," I told her.

"Bring me little water, Sylvie

Bring me little water now.

Bring me little water, Sylvie

Every little once in a while,

I think Lead Belly sang that," I said.

"Just once," I told her,
"I would like to go through a day
without having everything I do
come out in some old song somewhere
like Motown. Case in point:
if you want to know anything
about me just pull out some of those
old recordings and right there I will be.

Yap, those rascals, they got me."

She informed me that, "Many of those songs were
written long before you were even born.
I have no idea what you are talking about.
Lead Belly and that 'Jimmy Crack Corn' song

have never appeared on a Motown
recording anyway, that I'm aware of EVER."

Still, I did not care.

I had that Jimmy Crack Corn
song stuck in my head.
and that's all there was to that.

It's a catchy tune.

And Lead Belly was one of the greatest
12-string guitar pickers that ever lived.

What's more, I still groove to some of those old
Motown hits.

But what is there for one to do when
perhaps nowhere in the world
do the subtle enjoyments truly matter

except for in my head? And in there, what I say
goes if nowhere else.

Sometimes, though, things do break out from inside
disguised in the form of a song.

What the hell is a song anyway?

And can I help it if I can't remember where it comes
from or where it's been?

Who invented cheese? Do I care?

Obviously not.

"*Jimmy crack corn and I don't care.*"

By the way, that's in a Motown song.

Yes Sir-ee, bob, and Lead Belly did it,

as far as I'm concerned.

So there.

Cats of Our Lives

"The only escape from the miseries of life are music and cats."-Albert Schweitzer

The cats not contained by the inside
of our house are not
all together wild.
They just don't like the inside cats.

Reason: Unspecified.

"Hold a group meeting?" No. Unwise.

All the cats have scratched ears
and rubbed bellies.
All have snacks, water, and toys.
All have doors opened and doors closed
for them all the time.
And all but one has a tail.

The outside cats on the lawn are lazy dreamers
enough of them know how to sing.
But when it comes to marathon paw-licking

the inside cats really know their stuff.

I Do Not Remember Dancing

I do not remember
the pampas grass in Abilene
nor the Motown tune she said we danced to.
I recall we drove to the nadir of gasoline,
slept on a park bench,
split a dollar can of stew.

And the Motown tune she said we danced to
by cigarette-lighter-light and the moon
plus the park bench
and the dollar can of stew
revealed that we gathered sundry things about June.

By cigarette-lighter-light and the moon
I did memorize her face
and it was pleasingly
definite, the only competent thing about that June.

And though I do not remember dancing,
I did memorize her face
and it was pleasing
in how it curved around to make a nose.

Yet she, obstinate one, said we were dancing
in the hypothetical meadows of Abilene.

Case closed.

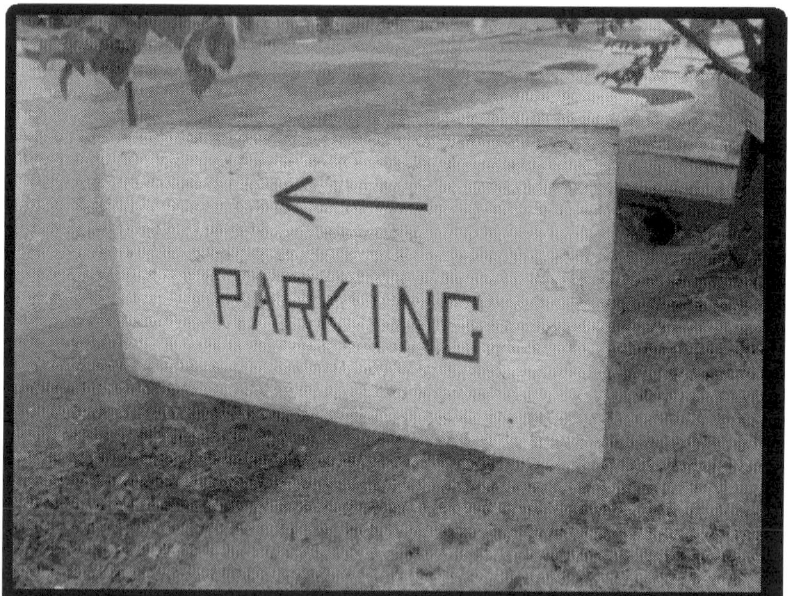
PARKING

John Lennon's Carpenter

There were many poets down on Harvard Square.
All had things to say and we said 'em too
that summer we stayed with John Lennon's Carpenter
and you threw up in his car.

And that's the closest to nobility that I have ever been
except for that time we spent at Walt Whitman's
house where I bought a poster and you wanted to sit
in his chair. I think that's the closest to nobility that I
have ever been.

We met up with an ol' jazz piano/journalism friend of
yours in Long Island. He said he'd show us New York
City and maybe catch a Broadway show.
He took us to 42nd street and a place where legend
had it, "Jack Kerouac threw-up in there."
Now that's the closest to nobility that I have ever been
in a land that heaves Walt Whitman's house,
John Lennon's carpenter, and yards of replaced
carpet.

Now what I have are these pictures of you on the
boulevard.
And here's one of you in a subway car.
And here's one of a friend of yours and mine showing
round these photographs
like this one of a Donald Roller Wilson's painting
of a Southern belle with a kitten head
(That's when we were passing through Arkansas)

That painting now hangs in the ranch-style home of
Carrie Fisher.

But as fine and well as all that summer was
I think that the closest to nobility that I have ever been
was my time spent with you
throwing up in the car of John Lennon's carpenter.

Walk Like the Sun

There are 1, 2, 3, 4
columns in this lobby
holding up what looks
to be the ceiling.

I am glad to not be one of them.

I count 6 fine chairs here, as well.
The chairs are holding up
what looks like human
rear ends.

I am glad I am not one of those.

I see 6 potted plants.
Someone has been taking good care
of them. Still,

I sure do not want to be a potted plant.

There is a neon light fixture overhead.
I would say it is about 12 feet long.

You know,
until today I have never thought much about being a
neon light.

I do not think I would want to be one.

This carpet, looks like, has not been walked
on much. It is gray but not as gray as
the Oklahoma sky specifically that
horizon place yonder where the sun goes down.

Some folks say it's that color
because of dust shaken from stars.
If the truth is told, I would like to believe them.

And even though this carpet is not the horizon,
I'm sure it has dust from some place or another
somewhere on it.

I will walk on this carpet as if I am the sun.

Look at me. I am walking

around the Earth like the sun.

Too Much Imagination

Last night, these hands
were cities
lined with streets
with towering finger mansions.

My right hand
was my metropolis.

The left:
it was more like just a hand.

But last night these
hands were cities.
I guess one hand should have been
a park bench

'Cause (and I should have known better)
it really hurt
when I tried walking
from one city to the other.

When Teri came home
and opened the door
I was stepping on both of my hands.

She looked at me as if the universe consisted of
nothing except maybe questions about itself.

Then she exclaimed,

"Tonight, Dear,
my hands are lobsters.

I'll be in the other room digging
for crabs, clams,
and mussels."

The Life of Me

Sombrero

Wind Blows, I've learned,
since I lost my sombrero
I wanted to burn.
Now mine is a hatless world.
But for the life of me,

I don't know what to do with these matches.

Sun Burns

Sun burns; it's true.
And except for my snowshoes
I run outside nude.
The neighbors tell me its winter.
But for the life of me,

I still really want the truth.

Chicken Switches

Watch synchronized,
I pull up my britches.
At last it is time
to flip chicken switches.
But for the life of me,

I don't know where they are.

At is Ket, At a Sket

At is Ket,
        At a Sket
                Abro Wnan dyel
           lowba Sket.
i WROTE
        Al et terto
        MyloVe
            An do nt(he)wa
                Yidr Oppe Dit.
Idr Oppe Dit
Idr Oppe Dit
            An do nt(he)wa
Yidr Oppe Dit.

i WROTE
        al et terto Mylo
Ve
            An do nt(he)wa
Yidr Oppe Dit.

Pie

"Sometimes it's like you're a big pie settin' on the table, and everybody runs up and gets their piece of you. When it's over, the plate's empty."
— Loretta Lynn

Now don't get me wrong, unless you think you must,
but pie is great— good as most manias get.
For how long do I crave pie? Long as it lasts.
Pie is for liking.

One sweet day, I would like to be like a pie.
I'd try hard to be good—as good as first-rate—
just like pie, and then pie and I could hang out.
I would so like that.

I seem drawn to a warm-on-window-sill
pie—temptation for wee mortals in passing.
And though I could be pie in a frozen box,
hot's still my first choice.

O how long till I knead the dough of summer?
When to lick spatulas of autumn and spring?
So where should I set the ovens of winter?
I dream and I dream.

But then I wake up from this feeling stupid.
I could never be a pie. I'm a mere man.
Pie is the pie. And I'm anything but pie
—far from scrumptious.

So I will fade away into un-pie-dom—
dessert-less—yet eating entelechy cakes.
Tell pie that I still like it. I always will.
I am just that way.

How to Offend a Fish

I tried tossing a stone into the lake
to mark a spot to leave some anger behind.
If things went right and nothing else went wrong
that stone should sink beneath the surface
and be forever hard to find.

(Okay, possibly a catfish might)

But the stone I picked proved too large.
And when I raised it overhead, I slipped first, then fell
into the mud. Gravity and the stone fell in next
onto my foot. Then the expletives began.
Glad nobody was around to hear 'em.

(Okay, a catfish did)

Great

Not that there was anything we could do about it,
you and I had lots of thoughts on our minds.

I was thinking of the rhododendrons
and how I could get a name like that.

You were thinking of the 5 cans of Spam
that fell from the shelves of Wall Mart.

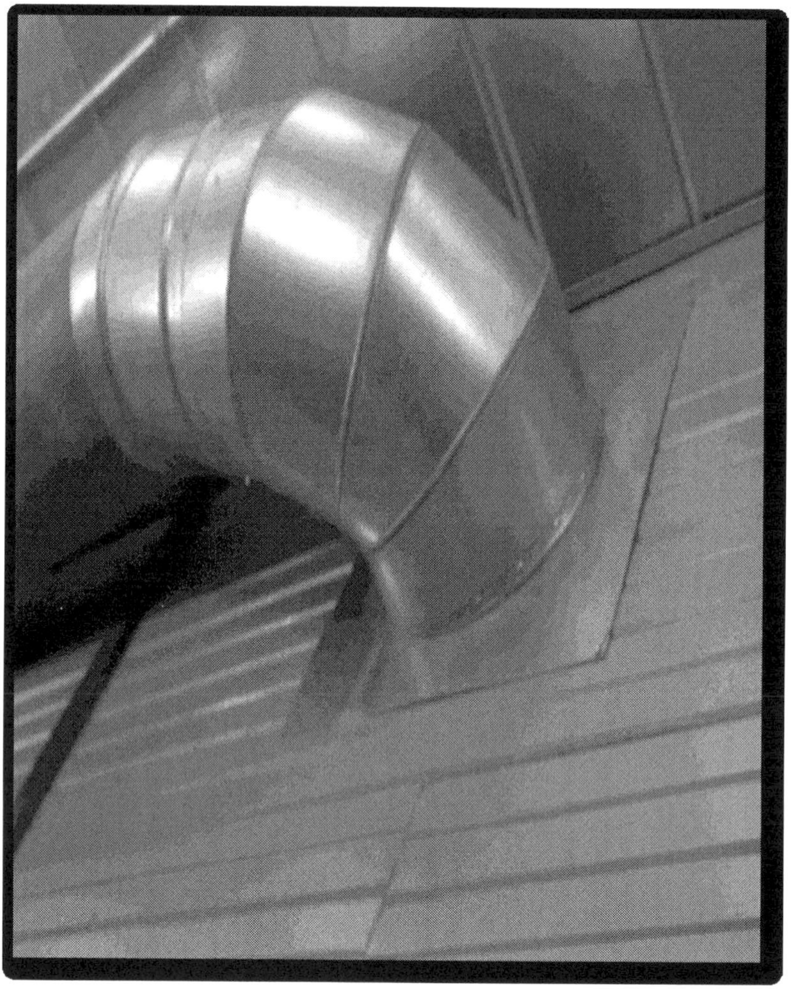

Friend,

Shut up.

Shh… We must speak in hushed tones.
Just act like tourists.
No,
no… don't point.
Goodness and mercy are following me all the days of
my life.
Lay low or they will find us.

I have no one else to turn to.
O, how this life has become such a shiny penny.
Yes, yes, I know–weep for me not–
but blue skies keep smiling at me.

And, hey, if tonight I become far too upbeat
to stomach, please, kill me.

My whole world has drawn closer to
wonderful and it orbits with excessive joy.
It's sad that it must shoulder all gleefulness alone,
so damn all this cheer to hell. My world
is the down-poured-on in a constant flood
 of springtime and fireworks.

O, when will my lips abandon all their whistling?
When will my feet not ache from all their skipping?

Why must I click these two tragically happy heels?
Why must I turn these cartwheels of bliss?

And don't tell anyone I told you this:

I, now and then, cease from my Motown-ing it
around the house
in order to glance out a window
where I watch and wait and wait.
I gaze toward heaven seeking out just one small
rain cloudy day with my name on it.
Why is it that I am still waiting?
I am waiting now.

And so friend, that's where you come in.
Because I can tell by the look on your face
and the tapping of your foot
that you could, in fact, care less.
There, you see, you are already nurse
easing the pain of my happiness.

I feel so walled in
by genuine love, compassion,
and charity all the time
that I am all but coconuts.

So lately I have been thinking of you
and how

you have been the one friend I can always trust
to be false, plastic, and condescending–much thanks.
I look forward to the continued benefit of your curses.

I so need someone to 'sick it to me' if ever I am low.
I need someone to pull the chair beneath me
if ever I change a light bulb or the sky.

And unto you, dear friend, I give a pencil,
one that you can jab into my eye if ever I should see
too much gladness in a universe filled
with far too much magic, wonder, and inspiration.

Here are 3 reasons why you are the friend who brings
me down:
1. You are the foot I trip over down life's staircases.
2. You are the knee I receive in life's woohoos.
3. You are the buckshot beneath life's wings.

You are my friend.

On Sunday

I mowed the lawn,
trimmed the hedges,
pickled cucumbers,
baked Alaska,
ate crow,
put an albatross around my neck,
fell asleep at the switch,
did some backseat driving,
put a bet on the wrong horse,
bit the hand that fed me,
built a castle in the air,
burned candles at both ends,
opened a can of worms,
put my cart before the horse,
crossed a bridge before I got to it,
went fishing for compliments,
hid a light under a bushel,
found out which side my bread
was buttered on,
locked the barn after
the horse was stolen,

made my bed and laid in it, too.

Garbage Can,
so open and receptive,

thank you.

And even though there
is not much we cherish together,

ugh, well,
someday, gosh…
how do I say this?

Do you think

maybe

sometime–

do you think I could take you out?

My Dream and Me

In my dream
I turned
around and all
idiots had vanished.

The world became
livable
for a change
for people
left behind.

Things were not so bad.
There were celebrations
— people liked it.

However,
I did not see me anywhere.

I looked
under everything

and
in every mirror.

I checked all the bars
and churches.

"What the hell happened to me?"

I wondered.

That's when I woke up.

Ignes Fatui

Seek not to absquatulate so often.
It does not sit you well in my company.

It's different, you know, when I busticate.
I'm good with divisions and with fractions.

Still, you gorgonize me thigmotactically
 — my hegira historically torpid like a Valonia.

So where goes a firefly when her light is out?
How shall a consonant wish for a vowel?

My name is Abasia. Your name is Abreact.
I am your denizen. You are never surfeit.

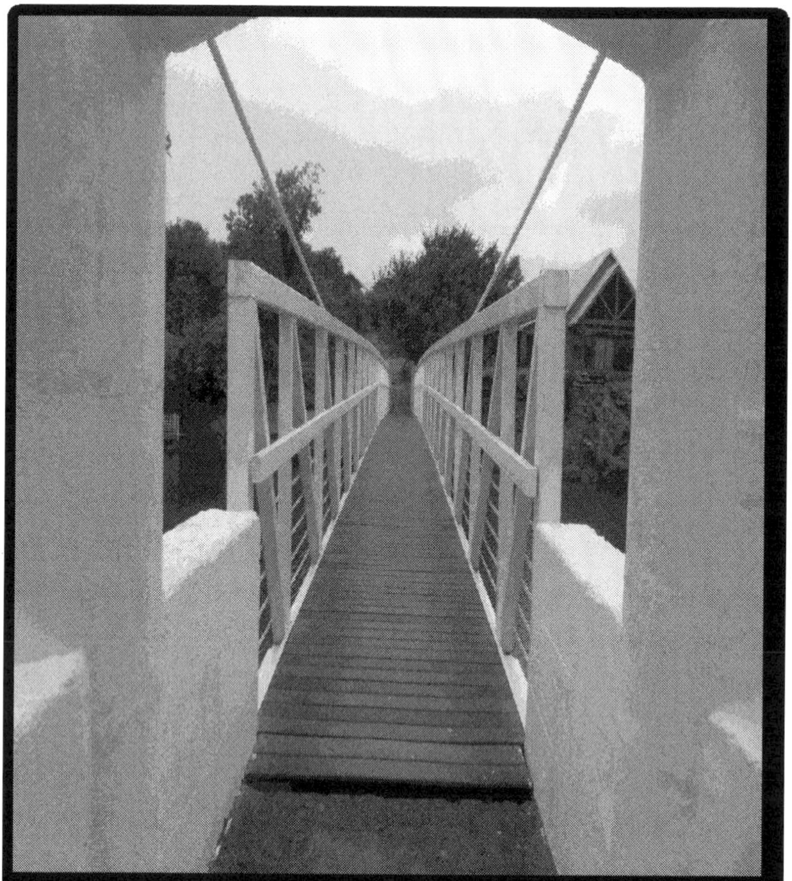

Notes of October

1.

My money does not shred
like all my other documents.
Why is that?

2.

My foot does not actually curse
the Earth
when it slams furniture
in the dark.

I must do all swearing.

Why is that?

I don't want to.

3.

Birds fly high
and fish swim deep.
And I'm stuck somewhere in the middle
looking up up at birds
--often on concrete streets
and in traffic.

If I'm near a river I get out
and look down down
at fish.

Why must I do this?

There are many things I do not understand today.
I wish I didn't have to.

Saturn has never looked better
That planet can see me well

Out here on my front porch swing
There are some stars over there

They don't seem to notice me at all
So I stick out my tongue at them

There is the half moon a-blushing
I just blew a kiss her way

She thinks I am, "Way too fresh."
Boy, I am glad the sun is not out tonight.

Not that the sun is poor company but
Some things just appear brighter now

Tonight, I will sit and swing on this swing
Since the pizza guy will not be here

For a while and I am not too hungry
And hey look, I just saw a falling star

One of the ones who only minutes ago
Was not paying much attention to me at all

I will eat one when it gets here — a
Slice of pizza, that is, in memory of that

One star. She behaves a lot like me.

Moon and Star

And you and I –*a moon*
Hope upon hope –*reflecting sun*
We throng together –*reluctantly*
Out of view -- *beyond horizon*
We're so conditioned –*behind the world.*

When the night be set about askew and the moon be a down *billedoux.*

And you and I –*a star*
We live –*falling*
We die –*beautifully*
Together –*passing*
We're so conditioned –*by the world.*

When the night when the stars be stewed

 –*merci beucoup.*

The Herman Imbroglio

There's a little girl
at school

—the bus driver brings her
and others much like her in
by the dozens

and lets them out—

and she somehow
knows
all the faculty's pets'
names by heart.

Yes, all of them.

'Wish someone
would have told me this
before I lied.

"Herman," I proclaimed

when she cornered me on the matter.

"Herman, the cat."

"How big is Herman?"

"Oh, about that big."

"What color?"

"Oh, brown and gray and black
with a white belly?" I lied.

Now, not counting
weekends and holidays,
three months have gone by.
Each morning, she asks me,

"How's Herman?"

"Just great," I say.

"Can you bring pictures?"

Things were going fine till she wanted pictures.

O how I wish I had never
invented the cat named Herman
because now I have to produce one.

And this little girl is sharp — she knows pets.

There's not a Rabbit, Snake, Ferret, Hamster, Poodle, Chihuahua,
Parrot, Iguana, Horse, Hermit crab, Emus,
Wildebeest, Chicken, Mule, Lama, Sea Monkey, or Pig
that she does not think about and truly love.

In other words, no other Herman will do.
She knows and loves Herman
far too much to accept
a substitute.

A cat matching Herman's description
should not be hard to find.
I must befriend him
and then photograph him.

There, you see,
I am making an effort
at becoming a decent person.

And oddly enough,

I am truly looking forward to meeting Herman.

Anaconda Freak 'em Caster (toot-a-doe and histo-blumder)

Abbie had a camera maker
form into a salamander.

Table blade for two and you can
throng and stringer and attack 'em lounder for
but a (a not b) was the saddle tarn.

Wobble downing ta wasb
a farnicorn lisb Ba.

Willie take Ur for jonden masterd
—a biz per globbin soundra?

No! It's faster, man, to vetida zap.

Then the news came.

Parnipper Zangerblast Derpintor Fan
was his name. And,
cABINTOR mapper Zinton was his game.

She asked him, "Why?"

He sat down to vapinsapple
when it all began.

Then Beor Loot Pond turned around
to see a pendleturn quark pindilke
zany middle sorp and
baked some dontor rector spin.

Alas...alas...zoomb!

Hecto twarn Castro pindleturn 40
carn zoot M&Ms?

She answered, "Ugh...New Jersey?"

He replied with nothing after
but many hampsters nibble streck
and babble napinsandador.

Hamble tonemantor gibbledon we now farewell

Hey, Hey hey.

"Go... Stop... Okay... Go," interrupted Ned
but then he had two.

Then, "Vu pnemocystic," Dr. M. J. Gaurd
responded with a smile,
"Caned, Zanodens Clod, such as, Got Mit, Jet, atom bomb Q."
as he failed them all single file but only for a little while.

So,
back to Anaconda Freak 'em Caster
only this time will it seem to lastama.

Who's to say bones and bones?

Oh...ooh.

Past the vista git him gotta urd quonimble zerox?
Comet or Cupid? Dominor or Blitzin?

Don't know. Can't blame 'em though.

The ban. It came and took our books away.
Said he came to check our vision gave us all a television.
Told them so but, Anacaonda Freecom Caster turned into a salad dancer.

A bee sat down to zimma
then zansaman spat in Abie's camera.

Ned jumped in, his next of kin,
we had to zappter him with gin.

Willie, taking a step, inquired,

"Is this the new carpet?"

"No," everyone said, "That's a shark."

As they took a holiday
took it alta all the way.

But all they really had to say was,

"A WARDIE MAN SITS, SIGNALS HIS BROTHER,

THEN BANGS HIM ON THE HEAD WITH A

RUSTY RAISIN."

Woman

Woman, your borough is sure though you toss
acorns from its spire at me.
Are not your kisses all here in Memphis?
Please, prep them for inspection. I'll wait
in the street and dance. I am a love target.

Sweetness, for the dulcet song I sing at you
I get a simper and an apian response I find confusing.
Perhaps yodeling it again will help with this?
And this time, Bob on kazoo will accompany.
Oh là là, this is the music my heart makes for thee.

Lady, for the mess you say my boots have made
upon your rhododendrons, please, commit me to the
prison of your love garden — your slammer of bliss.
From there I will send garlands sure to exonerate me.
I am green in your courtroom. This should account
for something.

Honey pie, I had only one fig in my pocket to share
with you tonight,
but the heat in this city has not been too kind.
Here it is, though, like love — a disorienting mush.
So come down here. Bring your hunger. We shall
feast.
Also, hurling things at me would be easier here in the
street.

Mistress of love that I am keen on, you as well as I know the daylight from the day and the nighttime from the night.
Yet, ah this knowledge — together we share — must for now
suffice since morning has brought with it

    a rain cloud,
    a paperboy,
    and a garbage truck.

And I wonder if they worship you as I.

D'ordinare

One day, I would like to be like a song
and I want Annie Lennox to sing me.
I would love to be notable like that.

One day, when it's way after midnight, honey,
I'm gonna rise up early like the sun.
I've always looked up to the sun. It's a great sun.

One day, I'm gonna stick my feet into the river
and I'm never gonna pull them out again.
That is if the fish and the mud don't mind.

One day, if I can remember to set a clock,
I gonna tell all people what time the train pulls out
so I won't have to do all the askin'.

One day, I'm gonna join in the summer of love.
I might even head down to Gaskers' farm
but, damn it, I'm already 40+ years late.

One day, I want to be Ella Fitzgerald's
great great grandson. I'd be great, yes I would.
I've always wanted to be great at something.

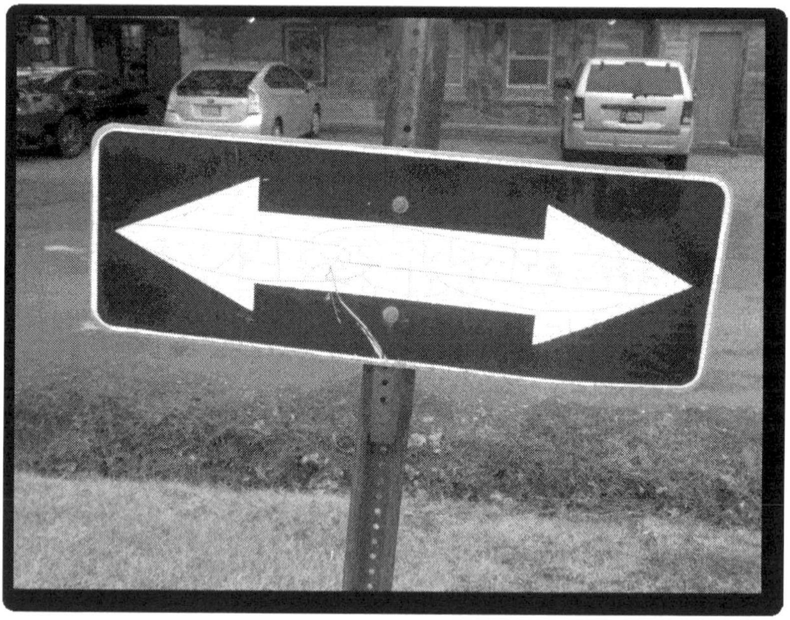

Still Life with a Cat

"Time spent with a cat is never wasted." — Colette

They came in electric
while I was trying to read a book
called, "Darkest England," by Christopher Hope.

And that was it.

I had to put the book down.

They began to holler

and then they began to cry out

and then they screamed

and then they shouted

and then they laughed at all things

and then they whispered

and then they pledged allegiance to something

and then they began to sing

and then they whistled Dixie

and then they frowned

and then they forgave themselves

and then they began to sneer

and then they found religion

and then they expressed amusement, mirth, and scorn

and then they sprang into action

and then they quibbled amongst themselves

and then they became lucid

and then they showed me some hemp clothing

and then they surprised themselves

and then they began to sing again

and then they over-threw the government

and then they wrote the great American novel

and then they lied to their parents

and then they came to their senses

and then they left

like they had been un-plugged.

I'm alone now...

There is quiet here...

Astronomical silence!

A cat enters...

Now I can get back to my book about Darkest England.

Then On That Same Night

Love is a snowmobile racing across the tundra and then suddenly it flips over, pinning you underneath. At night, the ice weasels come." —
Matt Groening

Then on that same night the sun refused to set.
I was not amused and I told the sun so.
You shook a finger like nobody's business.

That was a mistake.

The moon showed up with angry meteorites
and pissed-off comets. They were no match for us.
You put up your dukes — you were not at all kind.

And that's all it took.

The sun started to cry which started a chain
reaction till one by one the stars took to
flinging themselves from lofty constellations.

You held out your hands.

I thought, "This guy rides the bench in sports. As far
as catching things, he's been a symptom of health."
So then as the universe collapsed around us,

I had my concerns.

But I stood by you, friend, just to watch you fail
over and over again. I saluted
and I took off my hat in honor of you.

Then I crossed myself

as the Earth swallowed us up. Boy, was I mad.
I told the Earth so. You were also mad by
then — you, still trying to catch stars still falling.

That's when I woke up.

Fall to the Ground (tomber par ou a' tere)

Wrought from dirt and stones found
roughly everywhere,
as well as under everything,
the ground turns up apparent
where I stand.

It has been here these many years
and has become a fine footing.

I first met the ground at an early age
while faltering in learning how to walk
upright. I would try a few steps

—bam—

I would collapse.

Just why the ground would catch me,
I had no thought. Was I that valuable of a prize?

Life has been grand having had somewhere
to plummet.

The ground, I suppose, has stopped me
from descending
on down nowhere in particular past
insects, grass, roots, rivers, and worms
on down through the Earth's asthenosphere
and the center
of the earth's molten inner core
then out the asthenoshere again

out the other side past tree-tops, traffic lights,
birds, clouds, airplanes, and planets
—just myself drifting austerely
and eerily
out beyond ionosphere like so much
abandoned satellite debris.

Oh, I would not have forgotten
to wave farewell world.
I would have also stuck out my tongue
and made funny faces till I was no longer fun
anymore.

Eventually, my fate, I would cease to be a fascination
out there floating

because who am I kidding? I am not a spaceman—
I have never had much experience at hovering in
space.

I am in the universe enough already
right here on the ground.

On the ground *(en a' terre)*

if I fall to the ground *(tomber par ou a' terre)*

I feel an earth connection *(a' la terre)*

and that's not such a bad thing *(pas mal)*

One day *(un jour)*

I will meet the ground for good *(pour de bon)*

That will be the day I stop trying to translate this damn poem into French.

I'm not very good at it.

—*bonne nuit.*

Acknowledgements

The writer would like to acknowledge the influence of the following people: Sam McMichael, John Morris, Teri McGrath, Robert and Weyodi Swan, Dorothy Alexander, Jason Poudrier, Hardy Jones, Natthinee Khot-asa Jones, Cynthia Clay, Jennifer Long, Robert Miles Chisolm, Leah Chaffins, Jeanetta Calhoun Mish, Edward R. Romero, R. Darren Twohatchet, and Janie Lytle.

Another special thanks to Hoffman's Bar and Grill.